ANGULARJS

Easy AngularJS For Beginners

Your Step-By-Step Guide to AngularJS
Web Applications Development

Felix Alvaro

Acknowledgments

Firstly, I want to thank God for giving me the knowledge and inspiration to put this informative book together. I also want to thank my parents, my brothers and my partner Silvia for their support.

Table of Contents

Introduction

Hi there! Congratulations on acquiring this book. You have made a great investment in the attainment of new knowledge in AngularJS.

My name is Felix Alvaro and I am an Internet Marketer, Entrepreneur and Author with the mission to motivate and inspire you to achieve your goals, by sharing my knowledge and experience through my books.

For starters, I assume that what you led you here are one of these three things: you are interested in learning front-end development, you have just started learning JavaScript and your code has grown too complex that it takes forever to load, or you've finally had it with managing your 'spaghetti code' and you're ready to try something new. Whatever your reason is for your interest in learning AngularJS, I'm here to provide the basic knowledge to equip you with what you need to start your web app coding journey using AngularJS.

This book was written with the absolute beginner in mind but to understand AngularJS, you must have a basic knowledge of HTML, CSS, and JavaScript. If you haven't yet, I suggest that you learn JavaScript first. If you are new to JavaScript or don't know enough, I would strongly suggest that you go back and learn as much as you can. I have put together a great step-by-step guide that will teach everything you need to know and make you

feel confident to tackle AngularJS. To buy my best-selling JavaScript guide, click the image below or visit;
http://amzn.to/1mBhUYM

Getting started with AngularJS is fairly easy as long as you have a good grasp of JavaScript. In this guide, I am going to break everything down for you in a simple approach that will enable you to grasp everything quickly.

In the first chapter you will gain an understanding of what AngularJS truly is, its history, and its advantages compared to other JavaScript frameworks.

Let's get to it!

P.S Don't forget to claim your FREE Bonus video course at the end of this book. Enjoy!

Chapter One: Getting Started

Let's begin your web app development journey. To start off, let's discuss what AngularJS is, its history, and its advantages compared to other JavaScript frameworks.

What is AngularJS?

AngularJS is one of the many JavaScript front-end frameworks that have become popular throughout the years. When we say framework, this is where you build your application on. The framework dictates the structure of your code. But unlike other frameworks, AngularJS has notable advantages that make it standout from the pack. The AngularJS official website describes it as an enhanced, fully extensible HTML for web applications.

JavaScript frameworks were created to provide a more seamless end-user experience. When using a traditional server-side web application, any changes that the user makes initiates a page reload. If a user needs to click several buttons and to choose from a couple of drop-down choices, the user will be faced with a slow site that reloads each time a change is made.

Modern JavaScript frameworks are used in SPAs or *single-page applications*. To provide a better user experience, all the necessary code is provided within a single page load. What

JavaScript frameworks are capable of doing is to reload only the specific part of the page that the user is working on. This brings a faster user experience that users look for in a web application.

Aside from speed, traditional JavaScript/jQuery codes can become troublesome when it comes to code management. While this may work for small and intermediate complexity web applications, traditional web development can become a headache once your system expands and becomes a lot more complex than when you first started.

Here are a few of the most important qualities of AngularJS:

- AngularJS can be used to make Rich Internet Applications (a web application that is similar to a desktop application)
- AngularJS is an open-source and absolutely free framework currently maintained by Google.
- AngularJS is cross-browser compliant and supports the following browsers: Chrome, Firefox, Safari, iOS, and Android.
- The framework supports creating client-side applications using MVC pattern (more of this in the next sections)

History of AngularJS

Developers Miko Hevery and Adam Abrons created a side project that they called GetAngular in 2009. The name *Angular* was derived from the angle brackets < > used in HTML. The original vision for GetAngular was for it to be a tool that can connect to both frontend interface and backend system and it was originally intended for use by web designers – individuals who do not know how to program.

At that time, Miko Hevery worked for a project at Google. After six months of coding, he became frustrated when the code become too big at 17,000 lines) He and the rest of the team were having a hard time testing and modifying the code. Out of this frustration, Hevery used GetAngular, rewrote their project, finished rewriting it in 3 weeks, and produced only 1,500 lines of code. Because of this feat, his manager, Brad Green, grew curious of their side project.

One of the first big internal projects that used AngularJS was the rewrite for Google-acquired DoubleClick application. The project has shown tremendous success and from then on, Google has maintained the application. AngularJS is currently licensed under MIT.

Understanding MVC

AngularJS, including other JavaScript frameworks, utilizes the MVC design – or the *Model-View-Controller* software architecture pattern.

Let us breakdown the different parts of MVC to understand how this architectural pattern works.

Model – The model signifies data and the rules that govern data. For example, this can be a person's name, his email, and his birthdate.

View – Views are templates or the different ways on how the model can be presented.

Controller – The controller performs the necessary coordination with the server such as sending HTTP GET or POST requests. The model provides the controller with the information presented to the user and renders the appropriate view.

Here's a visual presentation of an MVC architectural pattern.

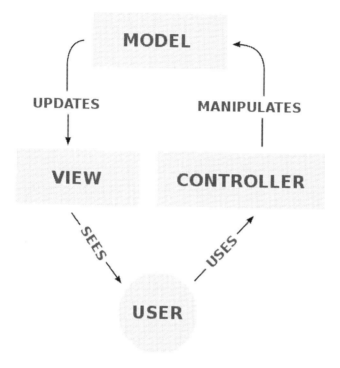

Figure 1 MVC Architectural Pattern

Let's use a real-world scenario. Let's say you we have an online clothing store. Users can either sign-up, browse for items of the same kind, search for all items offered by a brand, and purchase. If for example the user clicks on the Jacket category, the *controller* will receive this as an HTTP GET or POST request. The *controller* will then call the appropriate model and request it to return all jacket items. Once the model gets the request, it will retrieve the information from the data storage, run rules if applicable, and then return the list of jackets. Now that the controller has the information that it needs, the controller will decide the *view* that will be used or how the data will be presented to the user. If the user has personalized the background or is

11

accessing the page from a mobile, that particular view will be shown.

In terms of benefits, MVC architectural pattern provides a distinct separation between logic and interface. The model returns the same data regardless of where the information is viewed (desktop, tablet, or mobile). It will be the controller's responsibility to choose the appropriate template in showing the information.

Keeping the clear MVC segregation makes for better code management too. This allows for easier code updates, maintenance, reuse, and testing.

Advantages of Using AngularJS

As we've mentioned in the first part of this chapter, there are several popular JavaScript frameworks now: there's Backbone.js, Ember, and React to name a few. But why should you choose AngularJS among the others?

Here are some of the well-known advantages of using AngularJS:

- **Google!** The company's sponsorship on this open-source application signifies a stable and flourishing future for those who will switch to AngularJS.
- AngularJS can do **dual/two-way data binding** between *model* and *view*. It is possible to do automatic updates on both sides. Any changes in the *model* will be automatically reflected in the *view* and vice versa. This makes the web application more dynamic.
- Next, the **use of directives**. Directives are most essential in AngularJS because these create new syntax. Directives attach special behaviours to the DOM and extend HTML. I'll discuss more of this on Chapter 3.
- **Dependency injection** is responsible for speeding up development time. In simpler terms, DI means passing a service object to a client object. Instead of creating hardcoded values in the application, developers can create a dependency and then pass these to the component, effectively changing the output without spending too much time in coding.

Summary

In this chapter, we delved into an understanding of what AngularJS is, what it can do, and what are its advantages over other JavaScript frameworks. We also discussed briefly about what MVC software architecture pattern is and what are the benefits of using it. Now, you're ready to dive in and start with your first code!

Chapter Two: Your First AngularJS Code

In this chapter I will run you through creating your first code using AngularJS. I will also be showing you all the vital installations and breaking down all that you need to get starting with the code. Stay tuned.

Setting up Your Development Environment

To start coding, set up your development environment first.

There are 2 options that you can take:

- Try your hand at AngularJS using online editors. I prefer to use Plunker (https://plnkr.co/edit/?p=catalogue). For this book, you can use Plunker by copying sample codes to Plunker.

  Once you're on the page, click on the **Run** button at the top to see the output for the sample code.

Figure 2: Plunker Online Editor

- Setup AngularJS on your computer. To do this, download the AngularJS library. I'll discuss more in detail in the next steps.

How to download and install AngularJS

1. Go to the official website at https://angularjs.org/
2. Click on the *Download AngularJS 1* button.

Figure 3: Download AngularJS 1

3. A Download box will appear with the following options:
   a. **Legacy** or **stable** option – Click on the Stable option to download the latest 1.5.x version or the older legacy versions 1.2.x.
   b. Choose to download **Minified, Uncompressed,** or **Zip** files.

Download AngularJS

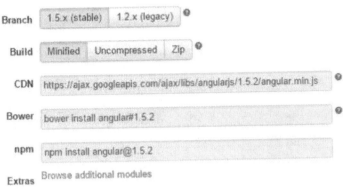

Figure 4: AngularJS Download

4. Once you've downloaded the AngularJS library, you
will need an editor such as Sublime Text
(http://www.sublimetext.com/) to start coding.

Here are quick Sublime Text installation instructions:

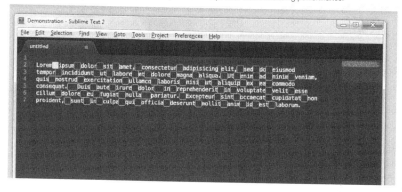

- Visit http://www.sublimetext.com/.
- Press *Download.*
- Follow the install Wizard.
- Move the application to your desktop for quick access.
- Done!

```
1   <!doctype html>
2   <html>
3
4       <head>
5           <script src = "https://ajax.googleapis.com/ajax/libs/angularjs/1.5.2/angular.min.js"></script>
6       </head>
7
8       <body ng-app = "sample">
9
10          <div ng-controller = "samplecontroller" >
11              <h2>Welcome to the world of {{helloTo.title}}!</h2>
12          </div>
13
14          <script>
15              angular.module("sample", [])
16
17              .controller("samplecontroller", function($scope) {
18                  $scope.helloTo = {};
19                  $scope.helloTo.title = "AngularJS";
20              });
21          </script>
22
23      </body>
24  </html>
```

Figure 5: Sample Code in Sublime Text

5. Make sure that you have browser where you can run
   your codes. I recommend using Google Chrome
   (http://www.google.com/chrome/) for all your web app
   testing – it's a plus too that both Chrome and AngularJS
   are maintained by Google.

   Once you have the code saved, go to Chrome, click on
   File then click on *Open File* and select the saved file.

   Here's the output when I ran the code above:

Welcome to the world of AngularJS!

Now, let's take the code above and dissect its parts.

```html
<!doctype html>
<html>

    <head>
        <script src = "https://ajax.googleapis.com/ajax/libs/angularjs/1.5.2/angular.min.js"></script>
    </head>

    <body ng-app = "sample">

        <div ng-controller = "samplecontroller" >
            <h2>Welcome to the world of {{samplehello.title}}!</h2>
        </div>

        <script>
            angular.module("sample", [])

            .controller("samplecontroller", function($scope) {
                $scope.samplehello = {};
                $scope.samplehello.title = "AngularJS";
            });
        </script>

    </body>
</html>
```

Figure 7: Sample AngularJS Code

The HTML part is where we define the AngularJS script file.

Next, the *ng-app* attribute signifies where the AngularJS content is contained. This attribute is usually combined with the *body* element as seen in our sample but it can also be used within the *html* and *div* element.

The next part defines which controller AngularJS should use. The controller is defined via the variable *ng-controller*. AngularJS will use the view defined in the HTML headings <h2> </h2> to show the model value supplied in *samplehello.title* parameter.s

The controller is defined towards the end of the script under the <script> tag. This part defines the controller named *samplecontroller* contained in the module named *sample*. The value of *$scope* parameter is now forwarded to the controller. Think of *$scope* as the model that binds the view and controller. All functions inside the controller are tied in the *$scope* concept. Don't worry if all information may seem fuzzy now. I will discuss more about these (controllers, directives, and scope) in the succeeding chapters.

AngularJS framework can be divided into 3 chief directives:

- **ng-app** – signifies the presence of AngularJS in HTML
- **ng-model** – Binds input controls to AngularJS data
- **ng-bind** – Binds AngularJS data to HTML tags

How To Use This Book

My goal in this book is to share all the basic knowledge that you will need to start coding in AngularJS. The book is divided into chapters and whenever applicable, each chapter will have a section for discussions, exercises, and output.

For simplicity, I will indicate only the AngularJS section and the corresponding HTML codes. Use the HTML section below and insert the codes where specified.

```
<!DOCTYPE html >
<html>
<head>
    <title>AngularJS for Beginners</title>
    <script src="http://ajax.googleapis.com/ajax/libs/angularjs/1.2.15/angular.min.js"> </script>
</head>
```

Figure 8: HTML Snippet

Summary

By the end of this chapter, either you should have already installed AngularJS or you have already familiarized yourself with online editors like Plunker. You have also seen a sample AngularJS code and an overview of its parts. You have also now seen your first AngularJS code. Let's continue on to the next chapter where I'll discuss more about AngularJS directives.

Chapter Three: Understanding Directives

In the first code in the previous chapter, you have already seen a directive declaration. But what are directives and how it is used in AngularJS? In this chapter, I will shed some light on one of the most important aspects of AngularJS - directives.

What are Directives?

Use of directives is one the most appealing benefit of using AngularJS. Directives create new syntax to extend HTML elements. Think of it this way: directives enable your regular HTML tags to level up and learn new skills. AngularJS directives start with *ng-*.

To understand the concept, let's discuss the built-in directives used in your first AngularJS code in Chapter 2.

ngApp

The ng-app directive signifies the start of an AngularJS code. This directive is defined anywhere where AngularJS should be active such as within *<html>*, *<body>*, or *<div>* tags. When defined within *<html>*, this means that AngularJS is used in the entire document.

Syntax:

```
<body ng-app = 'sample'>
...
</body>
```

Or

```
<div ng-app = 'sample'>
...
</div>
```

ngController

The ng-controller directive is responsible for specifying and handling data in the application. We'll discuss more of this in the next chapter.

Syntax:

```
<div ng-controller =
'samplecontroller'>
...
</div>
```

Some other major directives not used in your first AngularJS code are the following:

ngModel

This directive is used to define a variable that gets it value from user-input. In the example below, we're using model *foodname* to signify the value entered by user.

Syntax:

```
<div ng-app = 'sample'>
...
<p> What's your favorite food? <input
type="text" ng-model="foodname"></p>
</div>
```

ngBind

Another important directive in AngularJS is *ng-bind*. This directive binds or associates the user input to the model.

Syntax:

```
<div ng-app = 'sample>
...
p>ok, let's go out and eat <span ng-
bind="foodname"></span>!</p>
</div>
```

Directives Exercise 1

Now, let's combine all directives and see how it will work.

Open Plunker and paste the code below:

```
HTML Snippet here
<body ng-app="sample">
<h1>See how directives work</h1>
 <div ng-controller = "samplecontroller" >
 <h2>A conversation about
{{samplemeal.title}}!</h2>
 <p>what do you want to have for
{{samplemeal.title}}? <input type="text" ng-
model="foodname"></p>
 <p>Ok, let's go out and eat <span ng-
bind="foodname"></span>!</p> </div>
 <script>
          angular.module("sample", [])

          .controller("samplecontroller",
function($scope) {
          $scope.samplemeal = {};
          $scope.samplemeal.title =
"Dinner";
          });
      </script>
    </body>
 </html>
```

Output

Initial output will look like this:

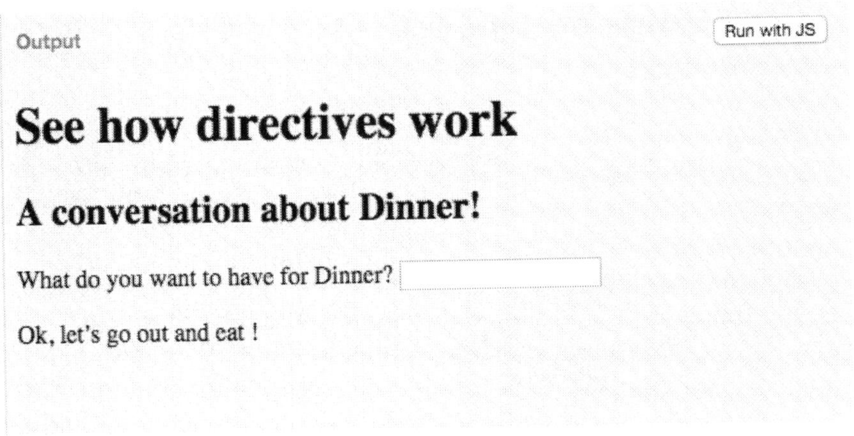

See how directives work

A conversation about Dinner!

What do you want to have for Dinner? [   ]

Ok, let's go out and eat !

Figure 9: Directives Exercise Output

Now, type a value for the input. Let's say we want to have *pizza*. Type the word in the text box. Once you type the word in, the output will be as follows:

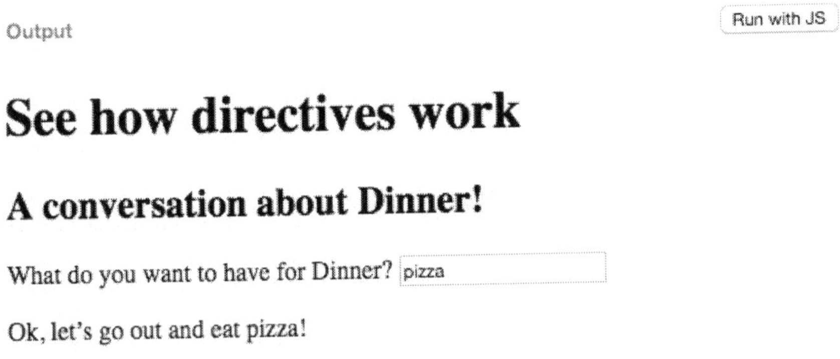

See how directives work

A conversation about Dinner!

What do you want to have for Dinner? [pizza   ]

Ok, let's go out and eat pizza!

Figure 10: Directives Exercise with User Input

Experiment with the values and see how the changes affect the output. Change the value for `scope.samplemeal.title` or change the `foodname`.

Built-in AngularJS Directives

The directives I've discussed above: *ng-app, ng-controller, ng-model,* and *ng-bind* are some of the basic directives used in AngularJS. To be fully in control of coding, you should also know some of the most useful AngularJS directives.

ngInit

This directive is used to assign values to variables in the form of an array.

Syntax:

```
<div ng-app = ""
ng-init="books=[{title:'Pride and
Prejudice',author: 'Jane Austen', genre:
'Romance'},
      {title:'Dracula', author:'Bram Stoker',
genre: 'Horror'},
      {title:'The Hobbit', author:'J.R.R
Tolkien', genre: 'Fantasy'}]"
</div>
```

ngRepeat

This directive is especially useful if you need to repeat the same HTML elements for a number of times. Note that there are several repeat expressions that can be used for *ng-repeat*. Repeat patterns are covered in intermediate and advanced AngularJS topics and not within the scope of this book. For now, let's use *item-in-items* pattern as specified by the ***book in books*** argument.

Syntax:

```
<div ng-app = 'sample>
...
<p> List of Books with Authors, and
Genre</p>
<ol>
        <li ng-repeat= "book in books"
            {{ 'Title:'+ book.title +
',Author: ' + book.author + ' ,Genre: '
+ book.genre}}
        </li>
</ol>
</div>
```

Directives Exercise 2

Now, let's put our theory to the test. Copy and paste the code below to Plunker.

HTML Snippet here

```html
<body>
<div ng-app="" ng-init="books=[
{title:'Pride and Prejudice',author:'Jane
Austen',genre:'Romance'},
{title:'Dracula',author:'Bram
Stoker',genre:'Horror'},
{title:'The Hobbit',author:'J.R.R
Tolkien',genre:'Fantasy'}]">
<p>What's your name? <input type="text" ng-
model="yourname"></p>
<p>Hello <span ng-
bind="yourname"></span>!</p> <p>Here are you
books:</p>
<ol>
<li ng-repeat="book in books">
{{ 'Title: ' + book.title + ', Author: ' +
book.author + ', Genre: ' + book.genre }}
</li>
</ol>
</div>
</body>
</html>
```

Output

Type in your name and see if you get the same output as below:

What's your name? John

Hello John!

Here are you books:

1. Title: Pride and Prejudice, Author: Jane Austen, Genre: Romance
2. Title: Dracula, Author: Bram Stoker, Genre: Horror
3. Title: The Hobbit, Author: J.R.R Tolkien, Genre: Fantasy

Figure 11: ng-repeat and ng-init directives

See how powerful directives are?

Here are some more directives that you might find useful:

Built-in Directive	What it Does
NgDisabled	Disables an element once the expression is evaluated to be true
ngClick	Used to specify behaviour once an element is clicked
ngKeydown	Used to specify behaviour on keydown
ngList	Used to convert delimited string to an array
ngReadonly	If expression is evaluated to be true, the element will be set to *readOnly*. User will be unable to edit.
ngSubmit	Directive that binds user input to onsubmit events
ngPluralize	This directive will allow you to adjust statements within your page depending on the number:

	For example, show any of the following messages whichever is applicable: *Nobody is viewing.* *1 person is viewing.* *{X} people are viewing.*
ngOpen	Directive used to open an element once the expression evaluates to true
ngRequired	This sets an element to a required state. Often used in conjuction with *input* and *select*
ngMaxlength	This directive will flag the maxlength error if user input exceeds declared maximum length

These are just some AngularJS built-in directives but if you want to know more about these and their capabilities, refer to the official AngularJS documentation guide for directives. (https://docs.angularjs.org/api/ng/directive)

If you are thinking of implementing a specific functionality, find out first if there are built-in directives that can suit your requirements. As I'd like to say when it comes to web development, there's no need to reinvent the wheel. If something in the system exists and is working great, use it.

However, it will be handy for you to learn how to create your own directive in case you can't find a built-in one.

Creating Your Own Directives

While AngularJS comes with built-in directives that you may find extremely useful in your program, there may be times when you need to make your own specific directive.

To create your own directive, you will need to use *angular.module* – a global function responsible for creating AngularJS modules/directives.

Let's create a directive that will add a line to every page or element that you add it to.

```
HTML Snippet here
<body ng-app="ownApp">
  <div> <h1> This is the first section
</h1> </div>
    <div sample-custom-directive></div>
    <div> <h1> This is the second section
</h1> </div>
    <div sample-custom-directive></div>
  <script>
  var ownApp = angular.module("ownApp", []);
  ownApp.directive("sampleCustomDirective",
function() {
    return {
      template : "<p>This is a directive
that adds this line</p>"
    };
  });
  </script>
</body>
</html>
```

Output:

Here is how the output will look like:

This is the first section

This is a directive that adds this line

This is the second section

This is a directive that adds this line

Figure 12: Creating Your Own Directive

In the code above, we have created our own *sample-custom-directive* using the global function *angular.module*. To invoke *sample-custom-directive*, we used the attribute way of doing it via the *<div></div>* tags.

Whenever you would need to use the *sample-custom-directive*, we can just add it to the HTML element.

Summary

The previous chapter discussed what directives are and how you can make use of both built-in and customized directives. This mechanism is one of the advantages of using AngularJS. Now that you've seen how directives are used in AngularJS application, let's proceed to the next chapter to discuss more about Controllers, including the *ng-controller* directive.

Chapter Four: Creating Controllers

After directives, let's have a look at AngularJS controllers, what these are, and how are they used in an AngularJS code.

What are Controllers?

In Chapter 1, I briefly discussed the MVC software architecture pattern. You've learned that the C part – *controller* – is the one that correlates the *model* (data) and the *view* (template). Controllers are simply JavaScript functions containing properties and other functions that are used within a particular scope.

What is a Scope?

The next question is: what is a scope?

In JavaScript terms, scope is an object that holds the *model* (data) that should be passed to the *view*. Scope uses the two-way binding mechanism of AngularJS.

Scope is represented by *$scope*. Controller will initialize the *model* as scope links the controller to the view.

Let's use simple examples to illustrate.

```
Driver Name = firstName: Max, lastName:
Green
```

These are simplified data for *Driver Name* – for simplicity purposes, we are just hardcoding a person's full name. In a real world scenario, *model* usually comes from a database.

```
<h2>Have a safe journey ahead
{{driver.fullName()}}!</h2>
```

The line above shows an AngularJS expression that will cover the *view* - how we want to see the *model*. The two lines of code can exist on its own and is not interdependent. How do we associate the *model* with the *view*? This is where a *controller* comes in.

Making Your Own Controller

In the next few lines, we will create a controller that will correlate our *Driver Name* data with the view.

```
function driverController($scope) {
    $scope.driver = {
        firstName: "Max",
        lastName: "Green",
        fullName: function() {
var driverObject;
driverObject = $scope.driver;
return driverObject.firstName + " " +
driverObject.lastName;
    } };
} </script>
```

Let's drill down on the details of how we created a controller:

38

1. First, we need to define a JavaScript function with *$scope* as an argument.
2. Define *$scope.driver* as a property of the *driverController* object.
3. Define *firstName* and *lastName* as properties of *$scope.driver* object. Assign default values.
4. Create a *fullName* function that will return the combined *firstName* and *lastName*.

Controller Exercise 1

Now that we have the complete MVC parts (M-*model*, V – *view*, C- *controller)*, let's put them together in a simple example. Paste the code below to Plunker.

```
HTML Snippet here
<body>
<div ng-app="" ng-
controller="driverController">
Enter your first name: <input type="text"
ng-model="driver.firstName"><br><br> Enter your
last name: <input type="text" ng-
model="driver.lastName"><br>
<br>
<h2>Have a safe journey ahead
{{driver.fullName()}}!</h2>
</div>
<script>
function driverController($scope) {
    $scope.driver = {
        firstName: "Max",
        lastName: "Green",
        fullName: function() {
var driverObject;
driverObject = $scope.driver;
    return driverObject.firstName + " " +
driverObject.lastName;
    } };
} </script>
</body>
</html>
```

When combined, we see a complete picture of the MVC architectural pattern.

First, we declared a *controller* using the *ng-controller* directive.

Model data is defined via user input. *driver.firstName* and *driver.lastName* are bound to the user input boxes.

View or template uses the *driver.fullName*, the result of the *fullName* function, and binds this to the *<h2></h2>* HTML tags.

Output

The initial output will be as follows – notice that the initial variables (Max Green) will be shown in the output.

Enter your first name: Max

Enter your last name: Green

Have a safe journey ahead Max Green!

Figure 13: Controller Sample Code Output

Modify the first and last name fields to see how it will affect the output.

40

Enter your first name: Bob

Enter your last name: Anderson

Have a safe journey ahead Bob Anderson!

Figure 14: User Input

Controller Exercise 2

Here's another example of a controller combined with the *ngRepeat* directive. This code accepts user inputs for a grocery list and prints the updated list.

```
HTML Snippet here
<body ng-app=''>
<div ng-controller="GroceryListController">
     Add to list:<input type="text" ng-
model="newitem"/>
     <button ng-
click="addItem()">Add</button>
     <h2>Grocery Items:</h2>

     <ul>
          <li ng-repeat="item in items"> {{
item }} </li>
     </ul>

</div>
<script type="text/javascript">
     function GroceryListController($scope)
{
        $scope.items = ["coffee"];
```

41

```
        $scope.addItem = function() {
        $scope.items.push($scope.newitem);
        $scope.newitem = "";
        }
    }
</script>
</body>
</html>
```

Again, let's identify the following:

- *model* – items from user input
- *view* – list of grocery items
- *controller* – take the new inputs (*model*) and adds it to the *view*

Output

Add to list: [   ] [Add]

Grocery Items:

- coffee

Figure 15: Grocery List Initial Output

Type an item in the input box and click the *Add* button. The list should be updated with the new item.

42

Add to list: [   ] [Add]

Grocery Items:

- coffee
- sugar

Figure 16: Updated Grocery List

Summary

In this chapter, you learned about what controllers are and what a scope is. You've also gained a working knowledge on how controllers are defined through a couple of exercises. The last two chapters about Directives and Controllers gave you an overview of how efficient AngularJS is. You are now ready to learn about more functionality! Let's start off with Expressions in the next chapter.

Chapter Five: Working With AngularJS Expressions

AngularJS expressions are powerful tools that you can use in your code. We'll discuss about the different expressions that you can use in this chapter.

What are AngularJS expressions?

AngularJS expressions are used to bind data to HTML. These are declared inside curly braces *{{expression}}* in an HTML element. AngularJS expressions are essentially JavaScript expressions except with the following differences:

- In AngularJS, you can use filters within expressions for data formatting. I'll discuss more about filters on Chapter 6.
- Expressions are evaluated for the *scope* and not in global like JavaScript does.
- Functions cannot be declared inside AngularJS expressions.
- Regular expressions are not allowed within AngularJS expressions.

Using AngularJS Expressions

Angular expressions can be used with numbers, strings, objects, or arrays. Here are the operators that you can use:

Operator	Description	Example
+	Addition (works for numeric and strings)	3+1
-	Subtraction	3-1
*	Multiplication	3*2
/	Division	6/3
%	Modulus (outputs the remainder of an integer division)	6%4
==	Equality	A==B // false
!=	Inequality	A != B // true
>	Greater than	A > B // false
<	Less than	A < B // true
>=	Greater than or equal to	A >= B // false
<=	Lesser than or equal to	A <= B // true

===	Strict equality (checks for the data type)	3 === 3 // true
		3 === '3' // false

!==	Strict inequality (checks for the data type)	3 !== 3 // false 3 !== '3' // true
&&	Logical AND	A && B // false
||	Logical OR	A || B // true
!	NOT	!(A && B) // true
b ? c : d	Ternary	
aKey = value	Assignment	Assigns value to key
anObject.aKey=value		Assigns value to object.key
anArray[]=value		Assign values to array
b | filter	Filter	Filter input b
b | filter1 | filter2		Use two filters filter 1 and filter 2 on input b
b | filter:arg1:arg2		Use arguments for filter

AngularJS Expressions Exercise 1

Let's have a look at what AngularJS expressions can do.

Here's a sample code that shows how AngularJS expressions are used:

```
HTML Snippet here
<body ng-app>
  <h1>Expression Samples</h1>
  <!--Arithmetic -->
  <p>6 + 4 = {{6 + 4}}</p>
  <p>6 % 4 = {{6 % 4}}</p>
  <!-- Using a JavaScript string method --
>
  <p>{{"Hello World".toUpperCase()}}</p>
  <p>{{"Hello World".toLowerCase()}}</p>
  <!-- Searching for an occurence of 'B' -
->
  <p>{{"brown".indexOf('w')}}</p>
  <!-- Ternary operation -->
  <p>{{1==0 ? "Red" : "Blue"}}</p>
</body>
</html>
```

Output

```
Expression Samples
6 + 4 = 10
6 % 4 = 2
HELLO WORLD
hello world
3
Blue
```

AngularJS Expressions Exercise 2

The previous exercise was a simple demonstration of AngularJS expressions but let's reuse one of our codes and add an expression to introduce a new functionality. We'll use the grocery list code from the previous chapter and add a counter.

```
HTML Snippet here
<body ng-app=''>
<div ng-controller="GroceryListController">
        Add to list:<input type="text" ng-
model="newitem"/>
        <p>Number of items:
{{items.length}}</p>
        <button ng-
click="addItem()">Add</button>
        <h2>Grocery Items:</h2>

        <ul>
            <li ng-repeat="item in items"> {{
item }} </li>
        </ul>

</div>
<script type="text/javascript">
        function GroceryListController($scope)
{
            $scope.items = ["coffee"];

            $scope.addItem = function() {
            $scope.items.push($scope.newitem);
            $scope.newitem = "";
            }
        }
</script>
</body>
</html>
```

Notice that we added the line *<p>Number of items: {{items.length}}</p>*. The *{{items.length}}* expression will be responsible for counting the number of items in the list.

Output

Type in items and click on add. The counter should increase with every item that you enter. Did you get the same results?

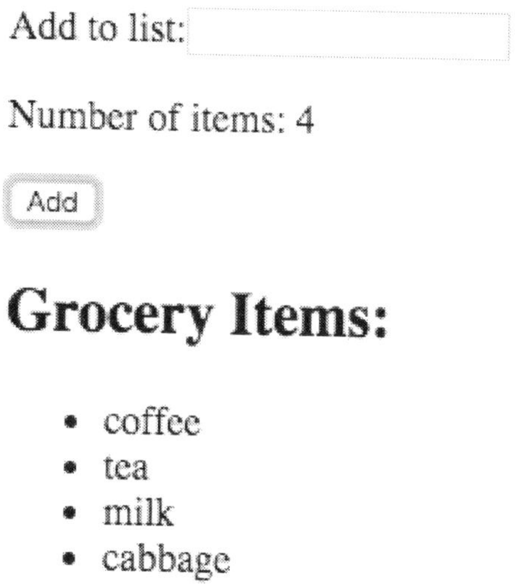

Add to list: [   ]

Number of items: 4

[Add]

Grocery Items:

- coffee
- tea
- milk
- cabbage

Figure 17: Adding expression to grocery list code

Check out the official documentation for AngularJS expressions at https://docs.angularjs.org/guide/expression.

Summary

In Chapter 5, we took a look into how AngularJS expressions are used and how these differ from JavaScript expressions. These were then supplemented with sample exercises showing how AngularJS expressions work. To further expand our understanding and skills in AngularJS web development, we will discuss Filters in the next chapter.

Chapter Six: Making Use of AngularJS Filters

What are filters? How do we use these in our code? These are the questions that I will answer in this next chapter. As you go on with the book, you should already be able to think of the ways that you can use different AngularJS functionalities in your code.

What are filters?

Filters are used to format data into what your code needs and allows you to control the presentation output shown in your views or templates. These are usually placed in directives or within expressions using the | or pipe character.

Some of the most common filters used in AngularJS are the following:

Filters	What It Does
lowercase	Converts the data case to all lowercase characters
uppercase	Converts the data case to all uppercase characters
filter	Filter the array based on a specific criteria and provide a subset
orderby	Arranges data into a specific order defined by the criteria

currency	Convert text to a currency format

AngularJS also provides many filters that you can use straight out of the box. As with built-in directives, find out if there's an existing filter that can give you what you need instead of creating your own code. It will save you both time and effort.

Using Filters

How do we use built-in filters? Let's take a look at sample codes used for different types of data.

Number Filter

Use the number filter to format numbers with specific number of decimal places or to round it off to x decimal places.

Exercise

Here is a code that will take user input for numbers. Use the code to test the number filter in formatting the numbers to present data with two decimal digits. The other example will show how *numbers* can round off up inputs to two decimal points.

HTML Snippet here

```html
<body ng-app=''>
  <div ng-controller="numberController">
    Enter a sample number:<input type="text"
    ng-model="sampleNumber"/></br>
    Enter a sample number with
    decimal:<input type="text" ng-
    model="sampleNumberDec"/>
    <h2>Filter for Numbers</h2>
    <p>Sample
    Number:{{sampleNumber}}</p>
    <p>Saomple Number with
    Filter: {{sampleNumber | number: 2}}</p>
    <p>Sample Number with
    Decimals Original: {{sampleNumberDec}}</p>
    <p>Sample Number with
    Decimals 2 places: {{sampleNumberDec | number :
    2}}</p>
  </div>
  <script type="text/javascript">
    function numberController ($scope) {
      $scope.sampleNumber = 100;
      $scope.sampleNumberDec =
    100.436783;
    }
  </script>
</body>
</html>
```

Output

Here is how the initial output looks like. The code will
compute for the initial values of 100 and 100.436783.

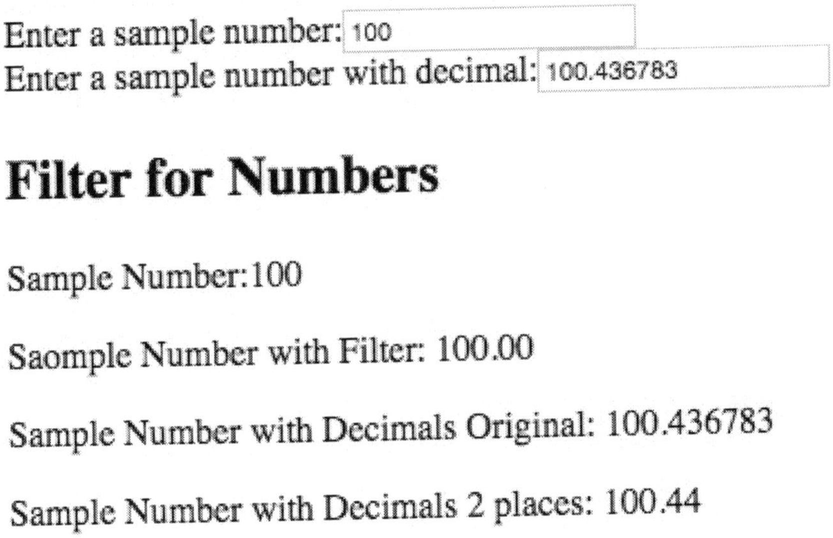

Enter a sample number: 100
Enter a sample number with decimal: 100.436783

Filter for Numbers

Sample Number:100

Saomple Number with Filter: 100.00

Sample Number with Decimals Original: 100.436783

Sample Number with Decimals 2 places: 100.44

Figure 18: Initial Output for Number Filters

To demonstrate further, enter other values in the *sample number* and *sample number with decimal* fields. Keep the *sample number* to a whole integer value to showcase the sample number filter function.

Enter a sample number: 37
Enter a sample number with decimal: 62.12673

Filter for Numbers

Sample Number:37

Saomple Number with Filter: 37.00

Sample Number with Decimals Original: 62.12673

Sample Number with Decimals 2 places: 62.13

Figure 19: Number Filters with User Input

Date Filter

There are a dozen possible ways to present data for date. Date filter in AngularJS allows you to present this information depending on what your application requires.

Here are parameters that you can use for date filter:

Date Filter Parameters	Sample Output
Medium	Jan 3, 2016 03:23:05 PM
Short	1/3/16 03:23PM
fullDate	Monday, January 3, 2016
longDate	January 3, 2016
mediumDate	Jan 3, 2016

shortDate	1/3/16
mediumTime	03:23:05 PM
shortTime	03:23PM

Exercise

Use the code below to see how you can use the date filter.

```
HTML Snippet here
<body ng-app=''>
  <div ng-controller="dateController">
    Enter your full name:<input type="text"
ng-model="fullName"/></br>
    When did you join the group? (yyyy-mm-
dd):<input type="text" ng-
model="sampleDateJoined"/>
                <h2>Date Filters</h2>
                <p>
Medium:{{sampleDateJoined | date:
'medium'}}</p>
                <p> Medium
Date:{{sampleDateJoined | date:
'mediumDate'}}</p>
                <p> Short
Date:{{sampleDateJoined | date:
'shortDate'}}</p>
                <p> Hi {{fullname}}! You
have joined the group in the month of
{{sampleDateJoined | date: 'MMMM'}} on a
{{sampleDateJoined | date: 'EEEE'}} at
{{sampleDateJoined | date: 'ha'}}</p>
            </div>
      <script type="text/javascript">
        function dateController ($scope) {
            $scope.fullName = 'John Green';
            $scope.sampleDateJoined = new Date
(2013,03,16);
        }
      </script>
      </body>
      </html>
```

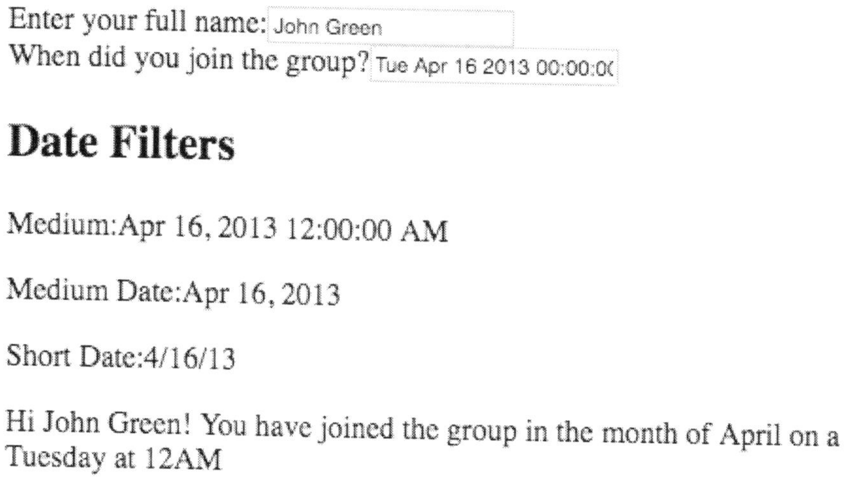

Enter your full name: John Green

When did you join the group? Tue Apr 16 2013 00:00:0(

Date Filters

Medium:Apr 16, 2013 12:00:00 AM

Medium Date:Apr 16, 2013

Short Date:4/16/13

Hi John Green! You have joined the group in the month of April on a Tuesday at 12AM

Figure 20: Initial Date Filter Output

Enter inputs in the data field and see how it affects the output. For the date input, enter a day in the YYYY-MM-DD format.

Enter your full name: Alex Lee
When did you join the group? 2013-03-11

Date Filters

Medium:Mar 11, 2013 12:00:00 AM

Medium Date:Mar 11, 2013

Short Date:3/11/13

Hi Alex Lee! You have joined the group in the month of March on a Monday at 12AM

Figure 21: Date Filter Output with User Input

Uppercase and Lowercase Filters

Next, let's discuss what one can do with strings. AngularJS provides *uppercase* and *lowercase* filters to format data.

Exercises

Here's a simple code to demonstrate both filters. Copy and paste the code to Plunker.

```
HTML Snippet here
</head>
<body ng-app=''>
  <div ng-controller="caseController">
```

58

```
        Enter your first name:<input type="text" ng-
model="firstName"/></br>
        Enter your last name:<input type="text" ng-
model="lastName"/></br>
                    <h2>Case Filters</h2>
                    <p> Original First Name:
{{firstName}}</p>
                    <p> Original Last Name:
{{lastName}}</p>
                    <p> LowerCase First Name:
{{firstName | lowercase}}</p>
                    <p> UpperCase Last Name:
{{lastName | uppercase}}</p>
                                </div>
    <script type="text/javascript">
     function caseController ($scope) {
            $scope.firstName = 'will';
            $scope.lastName = 'AndeRson';
     }
    </script>
    </body>
        </html>
```

Output

I've intentionally placed default values with different cases.
Most of the time, this can happen in real-life applications where
there could be differences in how users enter their data. The filters
can correctly display the user input.

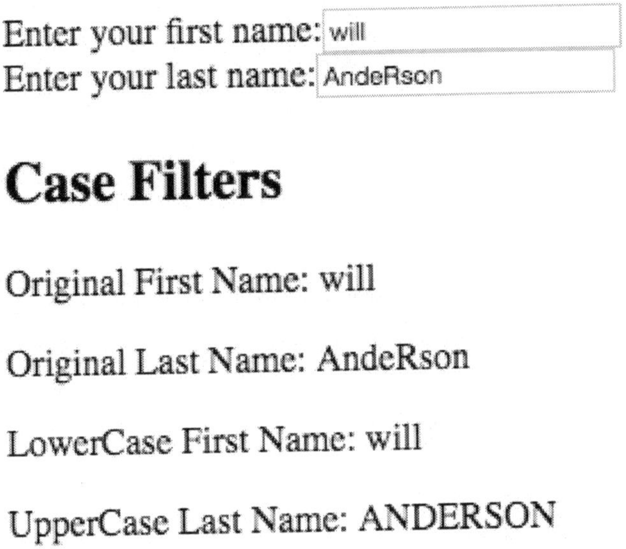

Enter your first name: will
Enter your last name: AndeRson

Case Filters

Original First Name: will

Original Last Name: AndeRson

LowerCase First Name: will

UpperCase Last Name: ANDERSON

Figure 22: Case Filters Initial Result

Modify the input to see how it will affect the results.

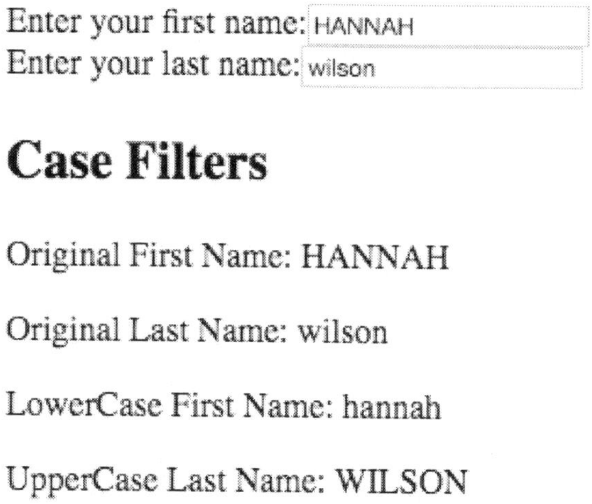

Enter your first name: HANNAH
Enter your last name: wilson

Case Filters

Original First Name: HANNAH

Original Last Name: wilson

LowerCase First Name: hannah

UpperCase Last Name: WILSON

Figure 23: Case Filters with User Input

Currency Filter

Another useful filter in AngularJS is the *currency* filter.

Exercise

This code shows how the *currency* filter is used and how it can transform data to reflect currencies.

```
HTML Snippet here
<body ng-app=''>
 <div ng-controller="currencyController">
```

61

```
        Enter a sample price with decimals:<input
type="text" ng-model="samplePrice"/></br>
        Enter a sample price (whole number
only):<input type="text" ng-
model="samplePriceWhole"/>
                <h2>Currency Filter</h2>
                <p>Sample Price:{{samplePrice |
currency}}</p>
                <p>Sample Price for Whole Number:
{{samplePriceWhole | currency}}</p>
                <p>Sample Price with round off:
{{samplePrice | currency}}</p>
                <p>Sample Price Whole Number with
other currency: {{samplePrice| currency: '£'}}</p>
                </div>
    <script type="text/javascript">
       function currencyController ($scope) {
           $scope.samplePrice = 100.446765;
           $scope.samplePriceWhole = 100;
    }
    </script>
    </body>
    </html>
```

Output

Enter a sample price with decimals: 100.446765
Enter a sample price (whole number only): 100

Currency Filter

Sample Price:$100.45

Sample Price for Whole Number: $100.00

Sample Price with round off: $100.45

Sample Price Whole Number with other currency: £100.45

Figure 24: Currency Filter Initial Output

62

You can also modify the code or the input data to change the output.

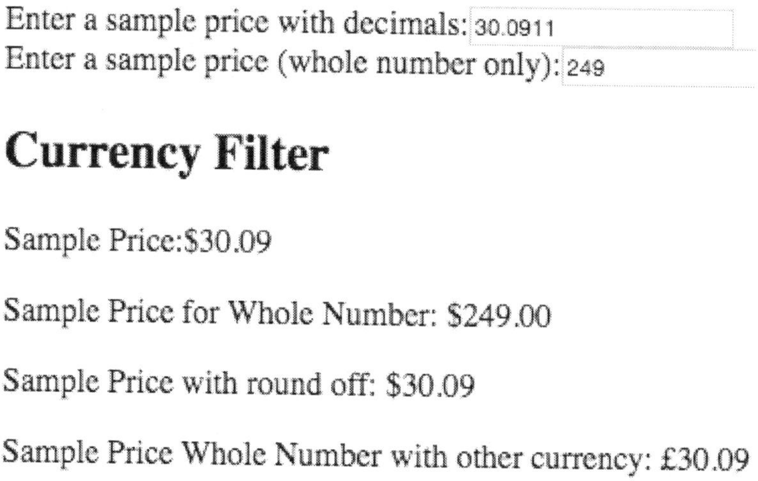

Enter a sample price with decimals: 30.0911
Enter a sample price (whole number only): 249

Currency Filter

Sample Price:$30.09

Sample Price for Whole Number: $249.00

Sample Price with round off: $30.09

Sample Price Whole Number with other currency: £30.09

Figure 25: Currency With User Input

Filter Filter

This is used to filter arrays to display only the data that passed the filter criteria.

Exercise

Filter is used in searching for specific text. Here's a short example of a search code using a hardcoded array.

```
HTML Snippet here
<body ng-app>
<div ng-init="books=[
{title:'Pride and Prejudice',author:'Jane
Austen'},
    {title:'Dracula',author:'Bram Stoker'},
    {title:'The Hobbit',author:'J.R.R
Tolkien'},
    {title:'Lord of the Rings',author:'J.R.R
Tolkien'},
    {title:'Summer Secrets',author:'Jane
Green'}]"
    </div>
    <label>Search: <input ng-
model="searchingFor"></label>
    <table id="searchResults">

<tr><th>Title</th><th>Author</th></tr></tr>
    <tr ng-repeat="book in books |
filter:searchingFor">
        <td>{{book.title}}</td>
        <td>{{book.author}}</td>
    </tr>
</table>
</body>
</html>
```

Output

Initial filter results will show all the contents of the array since we did not put any criteria.

64

Search: [   ]

Title	Author
Pride and Prejudice	Jane Austen
Dracula	Bram Stoker
The Hobbit	J.R.R Tolkien
Lord of the Rings	J.R.R Tolkien
Summer Secrets	Jane Green

Figure 26: Initial Filter Output

Now, search for the word *Jane* and see if the same entries as below would turn up.

Search: [Jane]

Title	Author
Pride and Prejudice	Jane Austen
Summer Secrets	Jane Green

Figure 27: Search Criteria 1

Searching for *tol* will pull up the results that contain the word *tol*. In our sample, it will return all the book titles from J.R.R Tolkien.

Search: tol

Title	Author
The Hobbit	J.R.R Tolkien
Lord of the Rings	J.R.R Tolkien

Figure 28: Search Criteria 2

Put *S* as your search criteria and the program will return all entries that contain an *s*.

Search: s

Title	Author
Pride and Prejudice	Jane Austen
Dracula	Bram Stoker
Lord of the Rings	J.R.R Tolkien
Summer Secrets	Jane Green

Figure 29: Search Criteria 3

See how great it is to use built-in filters?

Filters provide a way of manipulating and presenting data in a manner required by your application or your view templates.

For more information on AngularJS filters, read the official documentation at https://docs.angularjs.org/api/ng/filter.

Summary

In this chapter, you've learned what filters are and how they are used in a code. You've also seen samples of filters in action. In the next chapter, I will discuss AngularJS modules and what they mean to us as developers.

Chapter Seven: Understanding AngularJS Modules

Through the previous chapters, we've used the script function to contain all our code within the HTML file in the controller section. This is good for small codes and demonstrations but if you are thinking of launching a bigger application, you should be working on AngularJS modules for simplicity and for easier code organization. In this chapter, we will discuss what AngularJS Modules are and how we can use them in our code.

What are modules?

Modules are elements in AngularJS that are composed of directives, controllers, filters, and services. The diagram below illustrates modules in AngularJS. A single application can contain several modules that represent different logical functionalities in your app.

As you can see, a module can have different controllers and views defined within it. If you are running an e-commerce website, some of the modules that you might have are ones for Purchasing, Ordering, and Reporting. The number of modules can vary depending on the size and complexity of the application.

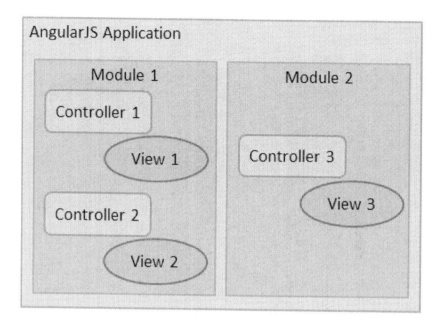

Figure 30: Illustration of Modules

To create modules, we use the *angular.module* mechanism. We also use this to invoke other previously created modules.

Creating Modules

Now that you have a picture of modules and what they can do, let's put the theory into practice. Do you remember our grocery list code? We will use that code and use a module to achieve the same results.

Here is the last code that we used:

```
HTML Snippet here
<body ng-app=''>
<div ng-controller="GroceryListController">
    Add to list:<input type="text" ng-
model="newitem"/>
        <p>Number of items:
{{items.length}}</p>
        <button ng-
click="addItem()">Add</button>
        <h2>Grocery Items:</h2>

    <ul>
        <li ng-repeat="item in items"> {{
item }} </li>
        </ul>

</div>
<script type="text/javascript">
    function GroceryListController($scope)
{
        $scope.items = ["coffee"];

        $scope.addItem = function() {
        $scope.items.push($scope.newitem);
        $scope.newitem = "";
        }
    }
</script>
</body>
```

To turn the code into a modular approach, we first need to define a new module. The code below creates the module *mySampleModule* and assigns the reference to the *mySamplemodule* variable. Paste the following lines of code into a file called *script.js*.

```
var mySampleModule =
angular.module('mySampleModule', []);
```

Next, we will use the variable we created to associate the controller to the module.

```
// use the mySampleModule variable to
// configure the module with a controller
mySampleModule.controller('
GroceryListController', function ($scope) {
        function
GroceryListController($scope) {
            $scope.items = ["coffee"];

            $scope.addItem = function() {
            $scope.items.push($scope.newitem);
            $scope.newitem = "";
            }
    }
    }
)
```

Here is how it is done on Plunker.

1. Click on the *New File* link at the left side of your Plunker screen. Create a new file with filename *script.js*

Figure 31: Create New .js File in Plunker

2. Copy the module code below to the *script.js* file.

```
var mySampleModule =
angular.module('mySampleModule', []);
// use the mySampleModule variable to
// configure the module with a controller
mySampleModule.controller('GroceryListContr
oller', function ($scope) {
        $scope.items = ["coffee"];

        $scope.addItem = function() {
        $scope.items.push($scope.newitem);
        $scope.newitem = "";
        }
    }
)
```

Figure 32: Put module code in .js file

3. Click on the *index.html* file and add the code below. Note that you should add `<script src="script.js"></script>` to your html `<head>` `</head>` tag.

At this point, your HTML head section should look like this:

```
<!DOCTYPE html >
<html>
<head>
    <title>AngularJS for Beginners</title>
    <script src="http://ajax.googleapis.com/ajax/libs/angularjs/1.2.15/angular.min.js"> </script>
<script src="script.js"></script>
</head>
```

Figure 33: HTML Head with reference to script.js

Copy and paste the rest of the code below to the *index.html*

```
HTML Snippet (with script.js
definition) here
```

```
<body>
    <div ng-app=mySampleModule>
        <div ng-
controller=GroceryListController>
            Add to list:<input type="text"
ng-model="newitem"/>
            <p>Number of items:
{{items.length}}</p>
            <button ng-
click="addItem()">Add</button>
            <h2>Grocery Items:</h2>

        <ul>
            <li ng-repeat="item in items">
{{ item }} </li>
            </ul>

    </div>
    </div>
    </body>
```

You should now have both *index.html* and *script.js* files in your Plunker screen.

Figure 34: HTML and JS files

Is the output the same as the one from our first code?

74

Add to list: [   ]

Number of items: 2

[Add]

Grocery Items:

- coffee
- tea

Yes, it is!

You have just seen how an AngularJS module works. Your .html file is simpler now and if ever you need to change a controller code, you will only need to work on the .js file. Modules provide a way to separate functions for easier debugging, troubleshooting, and code modifications.

For the sake of simplicity, we will be using modules whenever applicable throughout the remaining chapters of the book.

Summary

Modules make our lives easier. We're aiming for cleaner HTML files and modules provide a way to define JavaScript codes in a separate file outside of the HTML code. With the use of modules, we can organize codes more efficiently, troubleshoot faster, and modify codes without affecting other parts of the application. In the next chapter, we will discuss about services – a topic that we have not touched since the beginning of this book. Not to worry though! Since you already have a grasp of directives, controllers, and modules, services will be a breeze for you.

Chapter Eight: Exploring AngularJS Services

In Chapter 1, I stated **dependency injection**, or DI, as one of the advantages of using AngularJS. In this chapter, you will see the application of DI through the use of AngularJS services. In addition, I will talk about what services are, how to use these, and how can you create your app's own services.

What are AngularJS Services?

Services are independent JavaScript functions that are designed to do… well you guessed it, specific services. Controllers and filters can call AngularJS built-in services to perform designated tasks. Official documentation states that services are lazily instantiated meaning AngularJS only starts a service when an application requires it.

Here are some samples of built-in services:

Built-in AngularJS Services	What it refers to
$window	Browser's window object
$location	URL in the address bar
$document	Refers to the *window.document* object

Using Built-in Services

In the following sections, we will use sample codes to demonstrate how services are used.

$window service

$window refers to the *window* object. What happens when we define *$window* is that the framework instantiates the related service. In using services, note that we do not declare and start the service in our controller code, we simply invoke/ask for it.

This is an example of *dependency injection* wherein we do not need to declare a service within our code. We are simply asking for the value from the client object to be passed to the service object. We will see more of this in action once we create or own services.

Exercise

Here's a simple code to demonstrate how *$window* service is used in a code. Paste the lines below in their respective files in Plunker.

index.html

```
HTML Snippet (with script.js definition)
here
```

```
<body ng-app="mySampleModule" ng-
controller="windowController">
            <p>Window width:
{{windowWidth}}px</p>
    </body>
</html>
```

script.js

```
var windowModule =
angular.module('mySampleModule', []);
    windowModule.controller("windowContro
ller", function ($scope, $window) {
        $scope.windowWidth =
$window.innerWidth;
    });
```

Output

The output will display your current window's width.

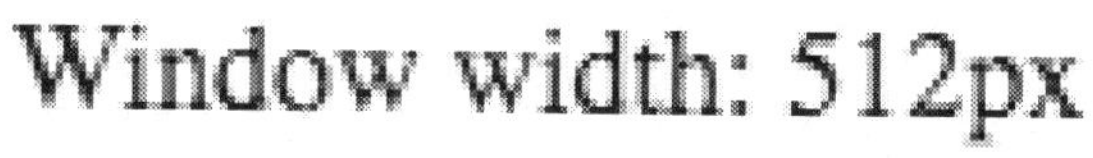

Window width: 512px

Figure 36: $window service output

Use other *$window* arguments if you wish to display other *window* object properties.

$location service

79

This service pertains to the *window.location* object and can be used to display the URL, the protocol, host, port number, and other *window.location* object properties.

index.html

```
HTML Snippet (with script.js definition)
here
<body ng-app="mySampleModule" ng-
controller="locationController">
        <p>The URL is: {{browserURL}}</p>
<ul>
    <li>{{browserProtocol}}</li>
    <li>{{browserHost}}</li>
    <li>{{browserPort}}</li>
</ul>
</body>
</html>
```

script.js

```
var locationModule =
angular.module('mySampleModule', []);

locationModule.controller("locationControl
ler", function ($scope, $location) {
                $scope.browserURL =
$location.absUrl();
                $scope.browserProtocol =
$location.protocol();
                $scope.browserHost =
$location.host();
                $scope.browserPort =
$location.port();
            });
```

Output:

80

The output will show URL *window.location* object properties requested in the controller.

The URL is: http://run.plnkr.co/q3QWtodFX1CzhR4e/

- http
- run.plnkr.co
- 80

Figure 37: $location service output

Use other *$location* arguments if you wish to display other *window.location* object properties.

$document service

This service points to the *window.document* object. Use this service to get *window.document* object properties. The code below will demonstrate its use.

index.html

```
    HTML Snippet (with script.js definition)
definition here
    <body ng-app="mySampleModule" ng-
controller="docController">
    <p>The page title is:
{{documentTitle}}</p>
```

```
          </ul>
         </body>
        </html>
```

script.js

```
      var docModule =
angular.module('mySampleModule', []);
    docModule.controller("docController",
function ($scope, $document) {
    $scope.documentTitle =
$document[0].title;
          });
```

Output

The output will show the page title as shown in the
window.document object.

The page title is: AngularJS for Beginners

Figure 38: $document service output

Use other *$document* arguments if you wish to display other
window.document object properties.

82

Creating Your Own Services

Most of the time, you will need to create services specific to your application. In the sample code that follows, we will create the service *ArithService* to multiply two given numbers.

index.html

```
      HTML Snippet (with script.js definition)
here
    <body>
    <div ng-app="mainApp" ng-
controller="MultiplyController">
    <p>Enter first number: <input type="number"
ng-model="firstNumber" /> </p>
    <p> Enter second number: <input
type="number" ng-model="secondNumber" /> </p>

        <button ng-
click="multiply()">Multiply</button>
    <p>Result: {{result}}</p>
    </div>
        </body>
    </html>
```

script.js

```
    var mainApp = angular.module("mainApp",
[]); mainApp.factory('ArithService', function()
{
        var product = {};
        product.multiply = function(a, b)
{
    return a * b
    }
        return product;
        });
    mainApp.controller('MultiplyController',
function($scope, ArithService) {
    $scope.multiply = function() {
```

```
    $scope.result =
ArithService.multiply($scope.firstNumber,$scope.
secondNumber);
      } });
```

To define a service, we first need to register the service factory function and the service name with an Angular module. We used the factory method to register the factory named *ArithService* that multiplies 2 numbers at a given time and the *service object product* returned by the factory function.

Next, we create the variable *product* to contain the results of the multiplication. The value of *product* is returned at the end of the function.

To set up the controller, we defined a new controller *MultiplyController*. This uses *$scope* and the new service, *ArithService*, as arguments.

Output:

Enter values for both input numbers then click on the *Multiply* button.

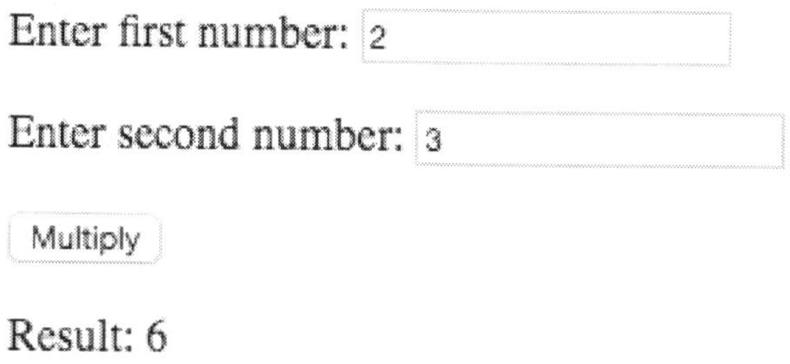

Enter first number: 2

Enter second number: 3

Multiply

Result: 6

Figure 39: AddService Output

An Overview of Dependency Injection

In the beginning of this chapter, we have established that *services* are one of the examples of the *dependency injection* mechanism within AngularJS. By the name itself, *DI* means that dependencies are 'injected' to components as opposed to the practice of hardcoding values within the component itself.

The following AngularJS components can be injected into each one as dependencies:

- Values
- Factory
- Service
- Provider
- Constant

I will provide one example for *dependency injection* using factory and service components.

In the previous section, you have learned how to use *factory* function to calculate and return a value. To demonstrate dependency injection, we will inject the *factory ArithService* to a new service called *ThriceService*. *ThriceService* will multiply any digit by 3. Once we inject *ArithService*, *ThriceService* will use the multiplication method within *ArithService* to come up with the results.

Copy and paste the following codes in the corresponding files.

index.html

```
    HTML Snippet (with script.js definition)
here
    <body>
    <div ng-app="mainApp" ng-
controller="ThriceController">
    <p>Enter a number: <input type="number" ng-
model="number" /> <button ng-
click="thrice()">Thrice the value</button>
<p>Result: {{result}}</p>
    </div>
    </body>
    </html>
```

script.js

```
    //create a factory ArithService which
provides a method multiply
    //2 numbers
    var mainApp = angular.module("mainApp",
[]); mainApp.factory('ArithService', function()
{
        var product = {};
```

```
                    product.multiply = function(a, b)
{
    return a * b
    }
            return product;
        });

    //inject the factory ArithService in a
service to use
    //the multiplication method within the
factory

    mainApp.service('ThriceService',
function(ArithService){
        this.thrice = function(a) {
        return ArithService.multiply(a,3);
    } });

    //inject the service ThriceService to a
controller

    mainApp.controller('ThriceController',
function($scope, ThriceService)              {
            $scope.thrice = function() {
            $scope.result =
ThriceService.thrice($scope.number);
    } });
```

Notice that the factory *ArithService* used in the previous
section to multiply any two given numbers has been reused in this
code. In the code above, we have used the same *ArithService*
factory to create a new function that gives out the result of three
times a number.

Output

Enter a value on the input field and click on the *Thrice the
Value* button.

87

Enter a number: 389 [Thrice the value]

Result: 1167

Figure 40: ThriceService Output

Unfortunately, other *dependency injection* methods are not covered in this book. If you wish to learn more about these, kindly check the official documentation at https://docs.angularjs.org/guide/di for supplementary reading.

Summary

Are you now convinced that *services* are one of the most flexible and convenient features of AngularJS? A well-designed AngularJS code makes use of services and the dependency injection mechanism in the most efficient way. Next, we will take a look into the different AngularJS Views.

Chapter Nine: Learning AngularJS Views

In Chapter 1, it is said that modern JavaScript frameworks are used in single-page applications. AngularJS allows SPA through multiple views on one page. Directives such as *ng-view* and *ng-template*, including the *$routeProvider* service, are used to support SPAs. In this chapter, we will take a look at how AngularJS handles single-page applications.

Installing the ngRoute Module

AngularJS does not come preinstalled with a *ngRoute* module. Prior to starting with samples for AngularJS views, you will need to download or install the *ngRoute* module whether you are using your local computer for testing or using Plunker and other online editors.

For AngularJS on Your Local Station

Visit https://angularjs.org/ to download. Once you see the download pop-up, click on *Browse Additional Modules*.

Download AngularJS

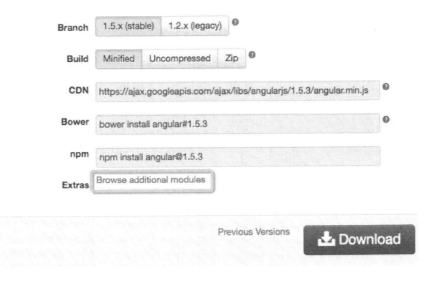

Figure 41: Installing ngRoute module

From the list, select *angular-route.js* or *angular-route.min.js*. Copy and paste the corresponding text file and save in your local AngularJS folder.

```
angular-messages.min.js.map
angular-mocks.js
angular-resource.js
angular-resource.min.js
angular-resource.min.js.map
angular-route.js
angular-route.min.js
angular-route.min.js.map
angular-sanitize.js
```

Figure 42: Download ngRoute file

Finally, add *angular-route.js* to your HTML <head></head> tags.

For AngularJS on Online Editor

For those using online editors, you just need to add scripts and stylesheets inside your HTML <head> </head> tags.

Your HTML snippet should now look like this:

```
<!DOCTYPE html >
<html>
<head>
    <title>AngularJS for Beginners</title>
    <link rel="stylesheet" href="//netdna.bootstrapcdn.com/bootstrap/3.0.0/css/bootstrap.min.css"/>
    <link rel="stylesheet" href="//netdna.bootstrapcdn.com/font-awesome/4.0.0/css/font-awesome.css"/>
    <script src="http://ajax.googleapis.com/ajax/libs/angularjs/1.2.15/angular.min.js"> </script>
    <script src="http://ajax.googleapis.com/ajax/libs/angularjs/1.2.15/angular-route.js"></script>
    <script src="script.js"></script>
</head>
```

Figure 43: HTML Snippet with ngRoute

Using the ngRoute module

The *ngRoute* module is responsible for providing linking and deep-linking directives and services for your AngularJS application. The module consists of the following components:

- *ngView* – directive
- *$route* – service used to associate controllers and views
- *$routeParams* – service used to fetch route parameters
- *$routeProvider* – service used when configuring routes

First, let's look at how routes are created. Defining routes will allow you to create a mapping for URLs and their corresponding view file names.

92

The code below instructs AngularJS that when the URL path is /LoginOldUser, it should load the view in login.html using the LoginController.

```
$routeProvider
//route for the login page
.when('/LoginOldUser', {
  templateUrl: 'login.html',
  controller: 'LoginController'
})
```

Let's say that we are creating the routing from the index.html page, the main page for our application. In this page, we will have links that would route us to the login page and the signup page.

We will do the code above for all the pages that you need to define routes to.

```
$routeProvider
//route for the login page
.when('/LoginOldUser', {
        templateUrl: 'login.html',
        controller: 'LoginController'
})
//route for the signup page
.when('/SignUpNewUser', {
        templateUrl: 'signup.html',
        controller: 'SignupController'
})
//catch all
.otherwise({
        redirectTo: '/LoginOldUser'
        });
```

We will then need to put the routes within a module with ngRoute as the dependency.

```
var newApp = angular.module("newApp",
['ngRoute']);
```

Let's put the script.js code together now complete with the module definition and controller definition.

93

script.js

```
var newApp = angular.module("newApp",
['ngRoute']);

newApp.config(['$routeProvider',function($routeP
rovider) {
                $routeProvider
                //route for the login page
                .when('/LoginOldUser', {
                        templateUrl:
'login.html',
                        controller:
'LoginController'
                })
                //route for the signup page
                .when('/SignUpNewUser', {
                        templateUrl:
'signup.html',
                        controller:
'SignupController'
                })
                .otherwise({
                //catch all
                    redirectTo:
'/LoginOldUser'
                });
        }]);

    newApp.controller('LoginController',
function($scope) {
        $scope.message = "This page will display
the login form";});

    newApp.controller('SignupController',
function($scope) {
        $scope.message = "This page will display
the signup form";});
```

For a simple demonstration of how routes work, we will use the simple HTML page below.

```
        HTML Snippet (with script.js, styles, and
ngModule) here
        <body>
        <h2>AngularJS Beginners Group</h2>
```

```
<div ng-app="newApp">
<p><a href="#LoginOldUser">Login</a></p>
<p><a href="#SignUpNewUser">Sign Up</a></p>
<div ng-view></div>
<script type="text/ng-template"
id="login.html">
            <h2> Login </h2>
              {{message}}
          </script>
<script type="text/ng-template"
id="signup.html">
<h2> Sign Up </h2>
{{message}}
          </script>
      </div>
   </body>
   </html>
```

Output

On the output page, the message for the *Login* page will initially be shown because we defined this as the catchall in our module code.

AngularJS Beginners Group

Login

Sign Up

Login

This page will display the login form

Figure 44: Main Page

Clicking on the *Sign Up* link will trigger the message for the Sign Up message. Toggle between the *Login* and *Sign Up* links to see how the output will change.

AngularJS Beginners Group

Login

Sign Up

Sign Up

This page will display the signup form

Figure 45: Sign Up Page

Here are some of the key points used in the code above:

- □$routeProvider is defined as a function of newApp module using the service '$routeProvider'.
- The $routeProvider.when defines a URL /LoginOldUser and /SignUpNewUser which are mapped to login.html and signup.html respectively. These pages should be found in the same path as main HTML page. In our case, since the HTML page is non-exsiting, we use the *ngTemplate* directive.
- The default view is set using the *otherwise* declaration.

- We set the corresponding controller for the view in the controller section.
- Notice that we used the *ngView* directive as part of a *<div>* element `<div ng-view></div>`. This directive is a placeholder for view configuration. It is responsible for including the rendered template of the route to the main layout of the page as defined in *index.html*.

Route Parameters

In the previous section, we have tried our hands at creating routes for a main page. The method that we used is to match the parameter *$location.path()* to an exact value. However, in cases when the application has several pages, say an e-commerce website with hundreds of product pages, it is not ideal (nor practical) to create a route for each of the product.

Imagine how tedious it would be if you have to create one route for each?

```
$routeProvider.when("/prod/11", { templateUrl:
"prod.html" });
$routeProvider.when("/prod/13", { templateUrl:
"prod.html" });
$routeProvider.when("/prod/506", { templateUrl:
"prod.html" });
$routeProvider.when("/prod/907", { templateUrl:
"prod.html" });
```

Fortunately, AngularJS allows us to simplify the configuration for these scenarios with the use of route parameters.

To demonstrate the use of route parameters, we will use the sample code for the Angular Beginners Group Login/Sign Up page.

First, we will create an additional page for members to contact the group. In the updated code, when user clicks on the *Sign Up* link, they will be given with two options: to sign up via email or to sign up via phone. Clicking on any of the links will take them to the Contact page. Instead of assigning two separate routes for the options, we will use route parameters instead.

To start, copy and paste below additional configuration for routes and controller in your *script.js* file.

```
// route for the contact page with choice
param
                    .when('/contact/:choice', {
                    templateUrl:
'contact.html',
                    controller:
'contactController'
        })


        newApp.controller('contactController',
    function ($scope, $routeParams) {
        var choice = '';
        if ($routeParams ['choice'] == "email") {
        choice = 'I want to sign up via email'; }
        else if ($routeParams ['subject'] ==
"phone") {
        subject = 'I want to sign up via phone';
        }
        $scope.choice = choice;
            });
```

In the code above, we have injected the service *$routeParams* as a dependency for the *contactController*. Next, we created the variable *choice* with a conditional logic to check for the values *email* or *phone*. If the user clicked on the *Contact the Group* link, the default value for *choice* (empty string) will be used. The service will enable us to extract the *choice* made by the user when he clicks on any of the links.

In the route definition, we defined a route for */contact/:choice*. The second portion of the URL path, *:choice*, signifies the value that will be supplied by the actual URL.

Next, add the following code to your *index.html* file. These codes are for the new Contact Page and it simply creates a form for sending a message. Note that is only a dummy representation and we will not be sending data to servers.

```
<script type="text/ng-template" id="contact.html">
<div class="jumbotron text-center">
    <h1>Contact Page</h1>
    <form style="width:25%;margin:auto;" role="form">
        <div class="form-group">
        <input ng-model="choice" type="text" class="form-control"
id="choice" placeholder="Subject"> </div>
        <div class="form-group">
            <textarea class="form-control" id="message"
placeholder="Message Us"></textarea>
    </div>
        <button type="submit" class="btn btn-default">Send
Message</button>
    </form>
</div>
</div>
    </script>
```

99

Let's proceed to modifying the Sign Up page to reflect the two ways users can sign up. Modify your HTML file with the configuration for your *signup.html* page.

```
    <script type="text/ng-template"
id="signup.html">
    <div class="jumbotron text-center">
        <h1>Sign Up</h1>
        <p>If you want to signup via email, <a
href="#/contact/email">click here</a>.</p>
        <p>If you want a fellow member to assist you on
the phone, let us know <a href="#/contact/phone">
        here</a>.</p>
    </div>
    </div>
        </script>
```

The code above uses two links */contact/email* and */contact/phone* that will both take the user to the contact page. The values *email* and *phone* are the possible values for *:choice* in the URL */contact/:choice* route definition.

This is how your final codes will look like:

script.js

```
    var newApp = angular.module("newApp",
['ngRoute']);
        newApp.config(['$routeProvider',
        function($routeProvider) {
        $routeProvider
        .when('/LoginOldUser', {
            templateUrl: 'login.html',
            controller: 'LoginController'
            })
            .when('/SignUpNewUser', {
                templateUrl:
'signup.html',
                controller:
'SignupController'
            })
            .when('/ContactUs', {
```

```
                          templateUrl:
'contact.html',
                          controller:
'ContactController'
                    })
                    // route for the contact
page with choice param
                    .when('/contact/:choice', {
                    templateUrl:
'contact.html',
                    controller:
'contactController'
        })
                    .otherwise({
                    redirectTo:
'/LoginOldUser'
    });
            }]);
    newApp.controller('LoginController',
function($scope) {
    $scope.message = "This page will display
the login form";
    });
    newApp.controller('SignupController',
function($scope) {
    $scope.message = "This page will display
the signup form";
    });
    newApp.controller('contactController',
function ($scope, $routeParams) {
    var choice = '';
    if ($routeParams ['choice'] == "email") {
    choice = 'I want to sign up via email'; }
    else if ($routeParams ['choice'] ==
"phone") {
    choice = 'I want to sign up via phone';
    }
    $scope.choice = choice;
        });
```

index.html

```
HTML Snippet (with script.js, styles, and noModule) here
<body>
<h2>AngularJS Beginners Group</h2>
<div ng-app="newApp">
<p><a href="#LoginOlduser">Login</a></p>
<p><a href="#SignUpNewUser">Sign Up</a></p>
<p><a href="#ContactUs">Contact the Group</a></p>
<div ng-view></div>
<script type="text/ng-template" id="login.html">
        <h2> Login </h2>
        {{message}}
    </script>
<script type="text/ng-template" id="signup.html">
<div class="jumbotron text-center">
    <h1>Sign Up</h1>
    <p>If you want to signup via email, <a
href="#/contact/email">click here</a>.</p>
    <p>If you want a fellow member to assist you on the phone, let
us know <a href="#/contact/phone">
    here</a>.</p>
</div>
</div>
        </script>
<script type="text/ng-template" id="contact.html">
<div class="jumbotron text-center">
    <h1>Contact Page</h1>
    <form style="width:25%;margin:auto;" role="form">
        <div class="form-group">
<input ng-model="choice" type="text" class="form-control"
id="choice" placeholder="Subject"> </div>
        <div class="form-group">
            <textarea class="form-control" id="message"
placeholder="Message"></textarea>
    </div>
        <button type="submit" class="btn btn-default">Send
Message</button>
    </form>
</div>
</div>
        </script>
    </div>
</body>
</html>
```

Output

For the initial output, notice that the only change you will
see is the new link to *Contact the Group* that will take users to the
contact.html page.

AngularJS Beginners Group

Login

Sign Up

Contact the Group

Login

This page will display the login form

Figure 46: New Main Page

Click on the *Contact the Group* link and see if you will get the same output as below.

You should see a form with a *Subject* and a *Message Us* field.

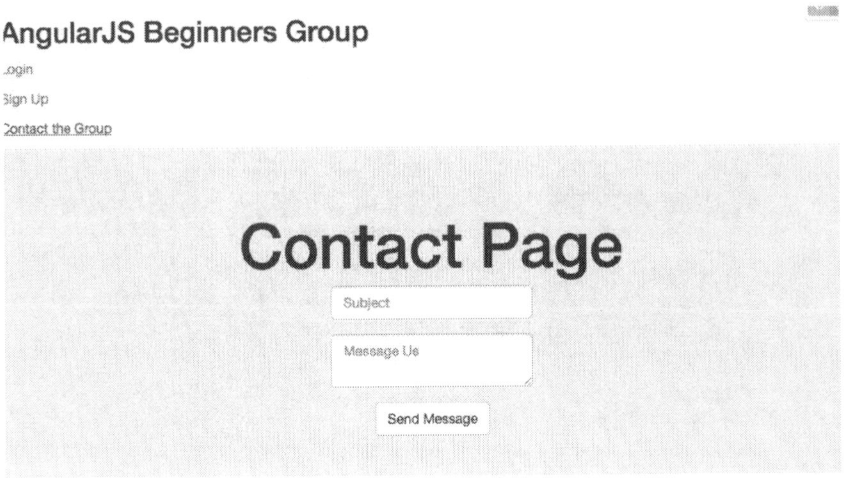

Contact Page

Subject

Message Us

Send Message

Figure 47: New Contact Page

Pay closer attention now, as this is where route parameters will be in action.

Click on the *Sign Up* link. You should now see the Sign Up form with the links for signing up via email or via phone.

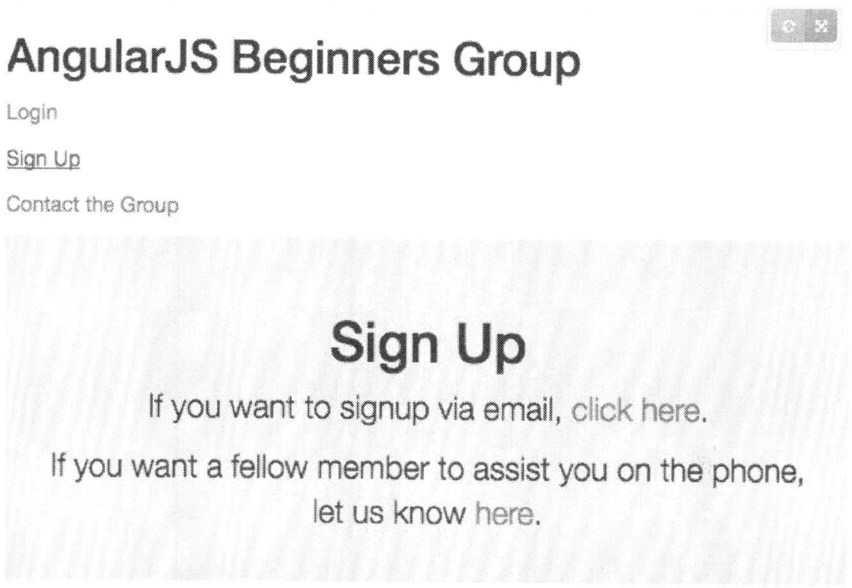

AngularJS Beginners Group

Login

Sign Up

Contact the Group

Sign Up

If you want to signup via email, click here.

If you want a fellow member to assist you on the phone, let us know here.

Figure 48: Sign Up Page Showing Two Options

Click on the *click here* email option and view the results.

The application should take you to the Contact Page with the Subject field populated with *"I want to sign up via email"*.

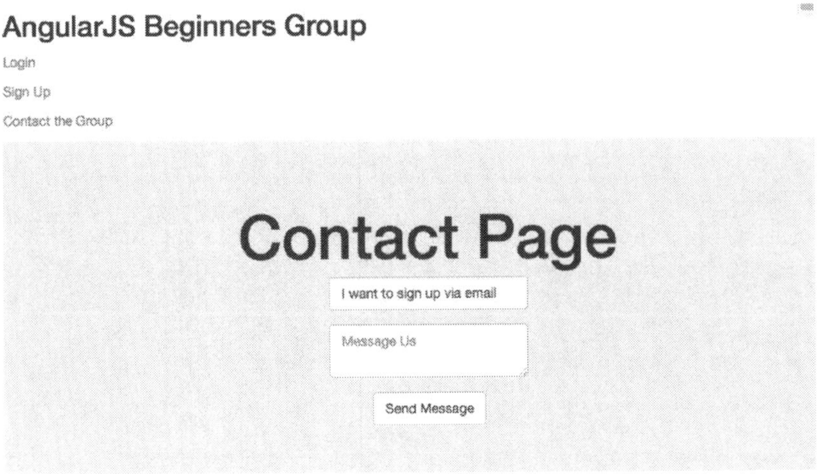

Contact Page

I want to sign up via email

Message Us

Send Message

Figure 49: Route for Signing Up Via Email

Now, click again on the sign up page and this time, choose the *here* link for the signup via phone option.

Notice that you will be taken to the same contact page but this time the subject reads, *"I want to sign up via phone"*.

Figure 50: Route for Signing Up Via Phone

That was quite a long explanation for how route parameters work but trust me when I say these will be your friend once your page gets bigger and bigger. Using route parameters also makes your corresponding HTML and script files easier to maintain; it's just a matter of copy and pasting the same configuration and updating previous ones with new links.

Summary

My goal in this chapter is to introduce you to how views are made within AngularJS. This chapter is not enough to discuss the subject in all its depth but I have provided you with the basic knowledge for you to start working on small projects. Again, the *ngRoute* module is an optional functionality that you can use in AngularJS. You can achieve the same results by putting the logic in the controller, however, if you want a cleaner code and one that is easier to maintain and troubleshoot, consider using AngularJS routing.

Here is a quick recap of what we covered in case you need a refresher on a certain step:

1. You now have an understanding of what AngularJS can do and what are its advantages over other JavaScript frameworks.

2. You now have an existing setup of AngularJS that you can use for your own projects.

3. You have learned about directives, how to use built-in directives, and how you can create your own.

4. You were introduced to controllers, how it is used, how scope relates to the controller, and finally, how you can create controllers for your own app.

5. You now know how to use AngularJS expressions in your code.

6. You are now familiar with what filters are and you can use the basic built-in filters in AngularJS.

7. You learned what modules are for and how modules simplify codes.

8. You have gained knowledge on what AngularJS Services are and how you can make services for your own app.

9. You have gained an understanding of the Dependency Injection mechanism.

10. You now know how to create view templates using the ngRoute module.

Final Words

In this book, I have provided you with the basic knowledge that you will need to start your journey in programming in AngularJS. The information that you have gained here in addition to your existing knowledge of JavaScript will help you create more efficient and easier to maintain codes.

In your further study, I recommend that you take on advanced topics such as troubleshooting and error handling in AngularJS, understanding other modules such as *ngAnimate*, *ngCloak*, and *ngInclude* (these are the modules that you start with), and exploring all the different ways that you can design and implement view templates.

Lastly, continue on practicing and taking small projects to start improving your skills. Through the knowledge imparted in this book, coupled with practice, you will be able to work on building your own websites or coding your own projects.

You may also consider learning other programming languages, your knowledge of AngularJS and JavaScript will give you a tremendous advantage if you wish to learn other languages. You can find other popular programming books by visiting our full library >> http://amzn.to/1Xxmab2

You can also join my email list to hear about new content releases as well amongst other cool stuff. As a thank you for joining, you will also receive part one of my popular video course

"25 Website Traffic Methods" where you will learn different methods to drive targeted traffic to your website or blog. To get access to the course, visit this link >> http://bit.ly/1PtpgK7

Finally, you can also send me an email if you have any questions, feedback or just want to say hello! (I do reply!) My email address is; (Felix_Alvaro@mail.com)

I thank you once again and God bless!

Before You Go, Here Are Other Books Our Readers Loved!

Learn JavaScript Programming Today With This Easy Step-By-Step Guide!

http://amzn.to/1mBhUYM

Learn Python Programming Today With This Easy, Step-By-Step Guide!

http://amzn.to/1WOBiy2

Learn Java Programming
Today With This Easy,
Step-By-Step Guide!

★★★★★

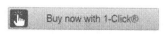

http://amzn.to/1WTgUw0

Learn R Programming
With This Easy,
Step-By-Step Guide

★★★★★

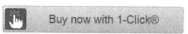

http://amzn.to/24XxoLM

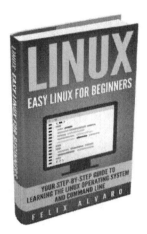

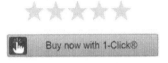

Learn The Linux Operating
System and Command
Line Today!

★★★★★

Buy now with 1-Click®

http://amzn.to/1QzQPkY

Learn C Programming
Today With This Easy,
Step-By-Step Guide

★★★★★

Buy now with 1-Click®

http://amzn.to/1Wl6fHu

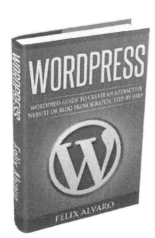

Made in the USA
San Bernardino, CA
25 June 2016